BUTTON and STITCH

Supercute Ways to Use Your Button Stash

by Kristen Rask

NORTH
LIGHT
BOOKS

CINCINNATI, OHIO
www.mycraftivity.com

13   12   11   10   09   5   4   3   2   1

Distributed in Canada by Fraser Direct
100 Armstrong Avenue
Georgetown, ON, Canada L7G 5S4
Tel: (905) 877-4411

Distributed in the U.K. and Europe by David & Charles
Brunel House, Newton Abbot, Devon, TQ12 4PU, England
Tel: (+44) 1626 323200, Fax: (+44) 1626 323319
E-mail: postmaster@davidandcharles.co.uk

Distributed in Australia by Capricorn Link
P.O. Box 704, S. Windsor, NSW 2756 Australia
Tel: (02) 4577-3555

Library of Congress Cataloging-in-Publication Data
Rask, Kristen.
   Button and stitch : supercute ways to use your button stash / Kristen Rask. -- 1st ed.
        p. cm.
   Includes index.
   ISBN-13: 978-1-60061-311-1 (pbk. : alk. paper)
   ISBN-10: 1-60061-310-1 (pbk. : alk. paper)
1. Button craft. I. Title.
TT880.R37 2009
745.58'4--dc22
                                    2009036588

METRIC CONVERSION CHART

to convert	to	multiply by
Inches	Centimeters	2.54
Centimeters	Inches	0.4
Feet	Centimeters	30.5
Centimeters	Feet	0.03
Yards	Meters	0.9
Meters	Yards	1.1
Sq. Inches	Sq. Centimeters	6.45
Sq. Centimeters	Sq. Inches	0.16
Sq. Feet	Sq. Meters	0.09
Sq. Meters	Sq. Feet	10.8
Sq. Yards	Sq. Meters	0.8
Sq. Meters	Sq. Yards	1.2
Pounds	Kilograms	0.45
Kilograms	Pounds	2.2
Ounces	Grams	28.3
Grams	Ounces	0.035

Editors: Tonia Davenport, Nancy Breen, Rachel Scheller
Designer: Steven Peters
Production Coordinator: Greg Nock
Photographers: Christine Polomsky, Dave Peterson
Stylist: Jan Nickum

www.fwmedia.com

DEDICATION

This book is dedicated to my mom and dad.

ACKNOWLEDGMENTS

I would like to thank my mom and dad; my sister Chelsea, and David; my Aunt Patty, Yasmeen, Misty and Uncle Farukh; and my wonderful group of friends including Lisa McGovern, Elena Moffet, Anna Links, Barbara Pronsato, Pamela Davis, Sandra Sikonia, John Yelsky, Nelson Harst, Kate Greiner and Aaron Murray, Depaz family, Cara Brooke, Coco Howard, Kevin Grady, Vicky Tamaru, Trisha Trent, Betsy Nordlander, Brian Layton, Candi and Spencer Hibert, Shawn Wolfe, Jessica Barnes, Angela Garbes, Anna and Peter David, Sally Brock, Sara Jane and Jeff Hoppe, Marci Lieber, Moxie, Colleen Beard and Lisa Burch.

A huge thank you to all the talented women who contributed to this book. Your creativity inspires so many people.

And lastly, to all the folks who read my blog and offer words of encouragement: The kindness of strangers will always amaze me.

CONTENTS

INTRODUCTION

Now and then, something just catches your eye. I am not a huge fashionista, but when a jacket or shirt draws my attention so that I can't stop staring at it, oftentimes it isn't the tailoring or the fabric that is truly fetching. It's the buttons!

Ahhhh, buttons. Everyone needs them, but not everyone appreciates them. This book is for those of us who do. Why buttons? My theory is that they often look like candy—and who doesn't like candy? They sound nice clacking across the table (not so nice clacking across the floor), and a handful feels good, like pebbles, seashells and endless possibilities. If buttons intrigue you, this book is your chance to make good use of the ones sitting in your coin dish, in your underwear drawer or on your craft table.

My own obsession started with a bag of buttons I found at a local thrift store. I was sewing a lot at the time and thought I might use them as embellishments. As I spilled them out onto my table, I noticed their differences in texture and color, size, shape and material. Mostly I noticed how much fun they were. I sewed one onto a piece of elastic and wore it as a ring. (You can do this, too; see page 104.) It garnered so many compliments that I made many more (hundreds at a time!) and sold them throughout the United States and Japan.

Six years later I have a collection of buttons that verges on the obscene, especially for someone living in a studio apartment. I also keep a special button collection beyond crafting purposes, reserved simply for appreciation. Most of them, however, have found new homes in various crafty projects, which brings me back to this book.

Button and Stitch is full of fun sewing projects that feature buttons as the main ingredient. Some projects are brought to you by yours truly, while many more have been contributed by talented people around the globe. You will find jewelry, home decor, accessories and so much more. You will surely sport buttons on all your goods in no time.

I hope you enjoy this book and find a new appreciation for the simple, versatile button.

BASIC MATERIALS

Here are some of the standard supplies used throughout the book. You can find most of these at craft supply and fabric stores, hardware stores and even your local grocery store.

Scissors: Purchase a good pair of fabric scissors and use them only for fabric. Mark them so everyone knows they are for fabric only. Your scissors will last much longer.

Needles: Keep both embroidery and sewing needles among your supplies.

Sewing thread: Each project indicates the type of sewing thread you'll need.

Embroidery floss: Choose good quality six-ply cotton floss.

Fabric: Fabric in all its colors, textures and prints is an obsession for many people (including me). The projects in this book use a variety of fabrics, but be sure to have some plain fabric on hand as well as some scraps of your favorites.

Adhesive: Use a strong adhesive. I prefer E6000.

Hot glue gun: A hot glue gun is one of those tools you will always be glad to have around.

Polymer clay: Polymer clay is inexpensive and comes in a range of fancy colors.

Jewelry tools: All you really need is a pair of needle-nose pliers to get started.

Sewing machine: You could make most projects by hand, but a sewing machine will save lots of time and energy.

Iron: Ironing fabric before use in a sewing project is a must!

Fusible webbing: Bonding fabrics together is easy with this product.

Ruler: Make sure your ruler has a smooth, clean edge.

Pencil: A pencil is a must-have.

Temporary and permanent ink pen: A temporary ink pen is really useful for marking work without ruining it.

Easy-tear stabilizer: Use this for embroidery designs—it allows you to stitch right through the stabilizer, then tear it away.

Each project also includes a materials list with tools and supplies you'll need to complete that particular work.

BUTTONS BY TYPE

Like many, you may have a small-to-large collection of buttons that you've accumulated over time—and although you don't want to get rid of your buttons, you really don't know what to do with them. If that's the case, this book is for you. There are many types of buttons, and soon you will most likely have your favorites. I am a big, BIG fan of Bakelite buttons, so let's start there.

BAKELITE

I love these so much because of the colors. If you're lucky enough to get your hands on them, you'll see what I mean. They come in all kinds of bright, bold colors to catch your eye. Bakelite buttons were most popular from the 1940s through the 1950s, but they have definitely made a comeback with collectors and enthusiasts.

ANTIQUE GLASS

Antique glass buttons are probably my second favorite type. Many in my collection are pretty small but have tons of detail. These also come in lots of fun colors and styles. Since they've become harder to find, it's really exciting when you do discover them.

WOOD

Wood buttons are one of my favorites to use for the base of my rings. They come in interesting sizes and cuts.

JET GLASS

In the late 1800s, when Queen Victoria went into mourning over the death of her husband, Albert, much of her wardrobe was made in black. She wore true jet glass, which had a huge influence on fashion during that period. Today, true jet glass is hard to come by. A good way to know if you have the real deal is by the feel. If the button feels warm, you've got yourself a winner.

ADDITIONAL TYPES

Often the mainstays of my button collection are made of "natural" material: mother-of-pearl, shell, leather, ivory, bone, metal and others. Some of these buttons are very easy to find, but it does not mean they are any less interesting or functional.

PART ONE:
BUTTON GIFTS

A certain joy comes with the act of giving a gift. You feel excited about the experience, anticipating the recipient's reaction and hoping your gift will be valued for years to come. As a recipient, there is nothing nicer than getting a gift you know was made specifically for you—a true gift from the heart.

This section is full of fantastic gifts you can make in a relatively short time without breaking the bank. Many of the supplies you need are basics you may already have. Some of these projects require a lot of buttons, while others require just a few wonderful accents. So break out your buttons and clear off that crafting space. Let's get started!

PEARLY BUTTONS FRAME

Taking a cue from seashell art or sailors' Valentine art, I decided to revamp and recraft an old frame with mother-of-pearl buttons. I used a group of mostly uniform buttons to create a clean, fresh look. You can purchase them in bulk from an online auction for just a few dollars.

Don't stop with frames, though. This same technique can be used with plain party trays, wood light-switch plates, clay pots and even pieces of furniture.

For a wilder effect, you could use buttons of all different colors and shapes. Look for large tubs of mixed buttons at fabric and craft stores.

Designed by Cathie Filian

Materials List

acrylic craft paint, neutral color (I used FolkArt brand in linen)

adhesive (such as E6000)

bamboo skewers (optional)

blank wooden frame with a flat front

mother-of-pearl buttons (flat, in various sizes — enough to cover your frame)

soft cloth or paper towel

paintbrush

putty knife or plastic knife

rubber gloves

small bucket of water

sponge

ultrafine grout (I used Mapei brand)

Step 1

Thoroughly clean your frame and allow it to dry. Paint the frame with a base coat of linen-colored acrylic paint.

Using the adhesive, attach the buttons to the base of the frame in a random pattern. Use a light application (it shouldn't be thick enough to overflow through the buttonholes onto the frame); it can be helpful to use a bamboo skewer or toothpick to apply the glue. Allow the glue to dry.

Step 2

Mix some of the linen paint with the grout. Add enough to make the grout the same color as the paint.

Step 3

Wearing rubber gloves and using the edge of a putty knife, spread grout over the buttons and frame. Work the grout between the buttons and let it set.

Step 4

Use a damp sponge to wipe away excess grout until the tops of the buttons are clean. Do not use a sponge that is dripping!

Set the frame aside to dry.

Step 5

Wipe off any grout from the outside edges of the frame and the edges of the opening. When most of the grout has been rubbed off, take a soft cloth or a paper towel and wipe the faces of the buttons to polish them.

Add acrylic craft paint to the edges of the frame and let dry.

Button Frame Variation

Using buttons that are all the same size, shape and material creates a completely different effect. The versatility of button frames allows for plenty of creativity, so use your imagination.

TIPS & TRICKS

You can remove the shank from a button with a wire cutter. Then sand the rough spots with a nail file.

FUN & EASY HEADBAND

This headband is fun to make because it can be styled in so many ways. You could make it for a special evening affair, a summer picnic or as an accessory for casual work attire. Use printed or solid fabric, and add as many or as few buttons as you like to give it panache.

Not only is this headband a fun and attractive addition to any outfit, it's also remarkably comfortable to wear.

Designed by Barbara Pronsato

 ## Materials List

three complementary graduated buttons if stacking; assorted buttons if sewing them across the headband

one 2½" × 19" (6cm × 48cm) piece of cotton batting

1"-wide (25mm) elastic (see page 18 for how to determine length)

one 2½" × 19" (6cm × 48cm) piece of striped fabric

one 2½" × 19" (6cm × 48cm) piece of black or white fabric

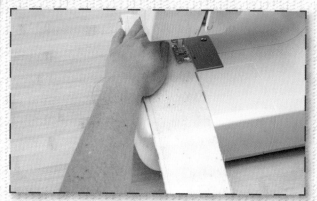

Step 1

Cut 2 pieces of fabric and 1 piece of cotton batting to 2½" × 9" (6cm × 48cm). Lay down the fabric with right sides together and the batting on top. With a ¼" (6mm) seam allowance, sew a straight stitch down both long sides.

Step 2

Turn the piece right side out and iron it.

Step 3

Turn the ends in about ¼" (6mm). Insert 1 end of the length of elastic, cut long enough to fit your head, under 1 of the turned fabric ends. (See box, right, to determine the length of elastic you'll need.) Sew back and forth several times over the turned end and the elastic to secure.

FITTING YOUR HEADBAND

When construction is complete, the elastic part of the headband should fit under the back of your head comfortably. To accomplish this, measure behind your head, lining up the measuring tape with your fabric, then add ½" (13mm) to the length of the elastic you cut for sewing.

Step 4

Insert the other end of the elastic under the turned fabric end and sew as you did in Step 3.

Step 5

Stack 3 buttons of graduated sizes and sew to the headband a bit off center. Or, as an alternative, sew assorted buttons across the face of the band. (See the headband variation below.)

Headband Variation

This sample demonstrates how easy it is to achieve a completely different look by changing the fabric and buttons. Imagine a whole wardrobe of headbands!

VINTAGE BUTTON BOUQUET

Unlike live flowers, these beautiful button blossoms last for years. Put a creative spin on the traditional wedding bouquet for a crafty bride, or give a bunch of button blooms to a friend or loved one to say "thinking of you" in a unique way.

Get out your favorite vintage buttons—it's time to pick a bouquet!

Designed by Lisa Jordan

 ## Materials List

- *assorted buttons (allow three to four buttons for each stem)*
- *18" (46cm) length of 18-gauge floral wire*
- *leather or other material for leaves*
- *leather needle (or sewing needle, depending on material)*
- *needle-nose pliers*
- *ribbon or length of twine*
- *wire cutter*

Step 1

Cut an 18" (46cm) length of 18-gauge floral wire. With needle-nose pliers, bend the wire at the center to create an elongated *U* shape.

Step 2

Thread on 4 buttons, starting with the smallest and adding progressively larger buttons. Buttons should be positioned at the center of the wire, with each wire end inserted through a separate hole on the button. For buttons with 4 holes, insert the wire into 2 diagonal holes.

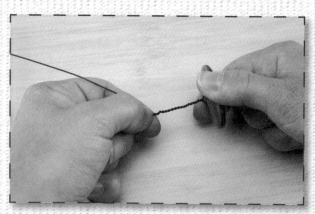

Step 3

Once you've stacked the buttons on the wire, pull both ends of the wire taut and twist them together. This creates the flower's stem and keeps the buttons from jiggling. Twist firmly at the base of the button stack (not too tightly or the wire will break), then continue twisting until the stem is the desired length. Snip the ends with the wire cutter.

Repeat Steps 1–3 for each flower in your bouquet.

Step 4

Cut 2 leaf shapes for each flower. Here, I've used a piece of recycled leather, but other materials, like felt, work well, too.

Step 5

To add leaves to the flower stem, punch a hole in each leaf with a needle, then thread the leaf up the stem to sit beneath the flower head (the button stack).

Step 6

Use needle-nose pliers to curl the ends of each wire stem back upon itself about ¼" (6mm) to avoid sharp ends.

Step 7

Continue to build stems until you have the bouquet you want. Gather and arrange the flowers, then tie them with a ribbon or a length of twine.

PINCUSHION-TOPPED BUTTON JAR

This button jar with a handy pincushion in the lid is a great gift for a favorite crafter or button collector in your life. Cute and functional, this item can be custom-made for the recipient with a stitched saying and specially chosen buttons.

Some ideas for the embroidered saying: *Buttons and Pins* (or *Pins and Buttons*), *Stick It*, *Button Up*, *Button and Stitch* or anything else you can imagine.

Designed by Kristen Rask

Materials List

assorted buttons (to embellish the pincushion and to fill the jar)

canning jar with lid (I used a Kerrs half-pint jar)

embroidery floss (colors of choice)

embroidery needle

¼ yard (23cm) fabric of choice

fiberfill

glue gun

pencil

straight pins

tear-away stabilizer

Step 1

On a piece of tear-away stabilizer, write what you wish to embroider on your fabric. Iron the fabric.

Step 2

With a pencil, trace the outside of the jar lid onto the back of the fabric. Cut out the circle, leaving about ⅛"–¼" (3mm–6mm) of fabric outside the pencil line.

Step 3

Center the stabilizer with the text on the fabric circle; make sure the lid rim won't cut off the letters. Secure the stabilizer with a couple of pins. Thread a needle with 1 undivided strand of embroidery floss. Knot the ends together to make a double strand. Stitch the text through the stabilizer. Here I am using a backstitch. I also like to use a variety of floss colors.

Step 4

Once you've embroidered the text, carefully tear away the stabilizer.

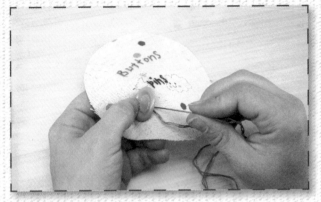

Step 5

Sew 1 or 2 buttons to the fabric for embellishment. Make sure the button(s) won't interfere with the lid.

Step 6

Center the removable lid insert over the back of the embroidered piece. Apply bits of hot glue to the lid seam in ½" (13mm) increments; wrap the excess fabric over the insert edge to adhere it to the back. Don't leave glue drips or globs or the lid will not close properly. The metal lid gets hot, so be careful not to burn yourself.

Step 7

When you are about halfway around the perimeter, begin adding fiberfill under the fabric. Continue to glue the fabric around the lid insert. You'll find it helpful to glue a bit, then stuff a bit.

Step 8

When stuffing is complete, push the insert into the ring of the lid. Pour an attractive selection of buttons into your jar and you're good to go!

PETALS & SPOOLS PINCUSHION

One thing every crafter wants and needs is a cute pincushion. Look no further; making this one is a cinch! Play around with the colors or add more buttons for a customized pincushion to keep or give.

Designed by Carol Grilo

Materials List

two buttons

elastic thread

embroidery floss

14" (36cm) square piece of fabric of choice

felt scraps for the appliqué

12" (30cm) square of foam

hot glue gun

interfacing

scissors

sewing needle and thread

straight pins

one small straw basket about 3½" (9cm) in diameter at the top

eight small thread spools

Step 1

Cut a 12" (30cm) square of cotton fabric. Cut a piece of interfacing a bit smaller and layer it over the fabric.

Step 2

Create a flower appliqué like the one in the photo from scraps of felt. Add a button to the flower's center. With a running stitch, sew the appliqué to the right side of the fabric, a bit off center. Sew through both the fabric and the interfacing.

Step 3

Cut a piece of foam into a square. Form the foam into a ball and hand-stitch the bottom to keep it from opening. Use a stronger thread, like embroidery floss, to help hold it together. Wrap the foam ball with the pincushion fabric, gathering the edges of the fabric at the bottom center of the ball. Stitch the fabric into place to secure.

Step 4

Apply hot glue to the inside bottom and around the inside rim of the basket. Insert the pincushion into the basket (with the appliqué on top) while the glue is still hot.

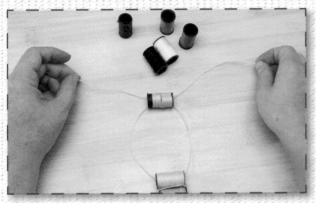

Step 5

To create a thread-spool bracelet embellishment for the outside of the basket, start with a 2' (61cm) length of elastic thread. Insert the thread through the first spool and center the spool on the thread.

Insert the ends of the thread into opposite ends of a second spool. Pull the elastic to "nudge" the second spool into position next to the first one.

Keep threading spools onto the elastic in the same figure-eight formation until all 8 spools have been strung.

Step 6

Thread the ends of the elastic back through the first spool and tie a knot to secure the bracelet together. Cut off any excess thread.

Stretch the bracelet of strung spools around the basket, evenly spacing the spools.

Step 7

To complete, secure a button to the center of the flower appliqué with a dressmaker's pin. Use additional pins for added embellishment.

BUTTON-BLOSSOM COASTERS

You can learn a few new crafty skills with this fun project. A little embroidery and crochet have a big impact on these cute coasters. (If you're not familiar with crochet and want to give the flower embellishments a try, consult a book on crochet instruction. The flowers use only three basic stitches: a slip stitch, a chain stitch and a double-crochet stitch.)

Select thread colors and fabric to match your home décor; or, if you're making these as a housewarming gift, take your color cues from the new pad. Protecting a table has never looked so good.

Designed by Kristen Rask

 ## Materials List

four buttons (I used identical buttons for this project)

cotton batting

crochet cotton thread in two complimentary colors

crochet hook size E

embroidery floss (colors that compliment the crochet cotton)

embroidery needle

felt

linen

pencil

scissors

sewing thread (colors to match the crochet cotton)

straight pins

tapestry needle

tracing paper

wool felt

Step 1

Using an existing square coaster, trace the outline onto a piece of tracing paper. Cut the square from the tracing paper. This is your template.

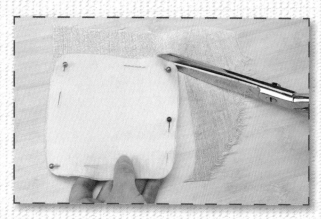

Step 2

Use the template to cut 4 squares from linen. With the same template, cut out 2 pieces of batting per coaster and 4 pieces of felt. (That's 4 linen squares, 8 batting squares and 4 felt squares total.)

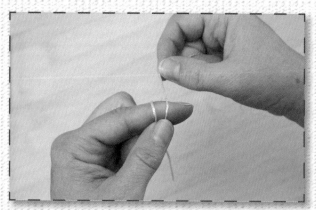

Step 3

To crochet the flowers for the coasters, start by wrapping crochet cotton (work directly off the ball) around your finger twice, leaving a 4" (10cm) tail.

Step 4

Ease the loops off your finger enough to insert a crochet hook through the ring (do not cut the crochet cotton). Thread over the hook from front to back and pull the thread through the ring—the thread should remain looped over the hook.

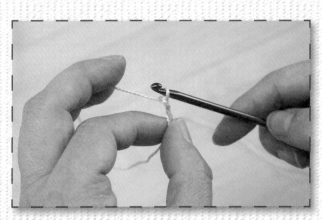

Step 5

Make a chain stitch: Thread over the hook again from front to back and pull the thread through the looped thread on the hook. This creates a new single loop on the hook.

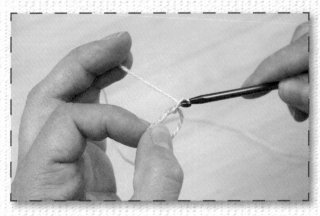

Step 6

Make a double-crochet stitch into the ring: Thread over the hook, then insert the hook through the ring. Thread over the hook again and pull the thread through the ring so you have 3 loops on the hook. Thread over the hook and pull the thread through 2 loops at once; thread over again and pull through the remaining 2 loops. This leaves 1 new loop on the hook.

Repeat until you have made a total of 15 double-crochet stitches in the ring. Pull the thread tail on the ring to tighten the ring.

Step 7

To close the ring of double-crochet stitches, slip stitch into the first chain stitch you made by inserting the hook through the chain; thread over, pull the thread through the chain and on through the loop on the hook. Pull up the thread so you leave a 4" (10cm) tail and cut the thread.

Use a tapestry needle to weave the 2 thread tails into the crochet work to hide them. Trim the excess thread.

Step 8

To make a second, smaller flower head, repeat Steps 3–7 with a different color of thread and make only 10 double-crochet stitches into the ring instead of 15. Thread an embroidery needle with the same color crochet cotton you used to make the large flower head. Stitch the large flower head to the upper left-hand corner of a linen square.

Layer the smaller flower head on top of the large one and stitch into place with matching crochet cotton.

Step 9

Sew a small button to the center of the flower. Repeat the entire process to make flowers for the other 3 coasters.

Step 10

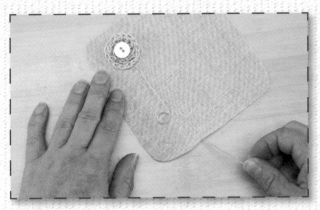

Thread an embroidery needle with 3 strands of green embroidery floss. Embroider a stem on each coaster starting at the base of the flower and working down about 1½"–2" (4cm-5cm). You can use either 1 long stitch or a series of backstitches.

Create 2 small leaves at the base of the stem. The leaves shown here are made up of small straight stitches. Refer to an embroidery book for other decorative stitches you may want to use for leaves, such as the daisy stitch.

Step 11

Make a sandwich with your fabric: Layer 2 pieces of cotton batting over the felt, then the embellished linen on top. Pin to secure the layers. Repeat for each coaster.

Step 12

Thread the embroidery needle with green embroidery floss (or use another, complementary color). Whipstitch* with diagonal stitches about ¼" (6mm) apart entirely around each coaster. To finish, knot the floss through the stitches on the bottom of the coaster and snip off the excess floss.

*For a different effect, you can use a blanket stitch to sew around the coasters.

SWEET HOME PHOTO ALBUM

Keeping pictures clean and organized can be a job in itself, but the results are worth the commitment. This project is gratifying to make because you can give it your own special touch with just a few minor adjustments. Change the drawing, add meaningful buttons and insert your favorite photos. This makes a heartfelt gift for many occasions.

Designed by Jacqueline Yeo

Materials List

assorted buttons

cotton batting (I used Warm & Natural)

embroidery floss

embroidery needle

one piece colored fabric, same height as cover fabric

one piece neutral cotton fabric (for cover; see page 40 for instructions on determining the size)

one piece lining fabric, same size as cover fabric

scraps of colored fabric

lace, ribbon or other trim

pencil

photo pages insert

seam ripper

scissors

sewing machine

sewing thread

straight pins

tear-away stabilizer

Step 1

Sketch out a design for the front of the album on tear-away stabilizer. Use the photos that will fill the album as inspiration or even the shape of the buttons or lace you've collected. (My album contained snapshots taken around the house, hence the shape.) A design with simple shapes and silhouettes works best. Note the shapes you'll want to cut out for the reverse appliqué, such as windows in the house.

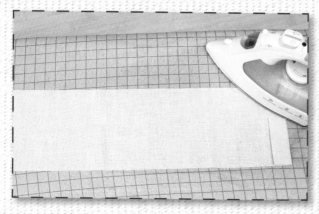

Step 2

Open the photo pages insert so it lies flat; measure the length and the height. Add 10" (25cm) to the length and 1" (25mm) to the height; this is the raw measurement of your cover. Cut a piece of lining fabric to this size.

Cut a piece of cover fabric to the same measurement, but stitch a patch of colored fabric to the right end. Trim this sewn piece to the correct measurement for the cover. Turn both cover ends under ½" (13mm) and iron. Fold the colored fabric under an additional 1" (25mm) and iron again. Machine-stitch each end to finish.

Step 3

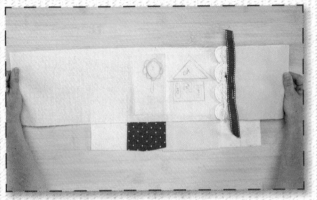

Lay out the cover fabric with the turned ends folded under (the end with the colored fabric should be on the right). Working from the center over the right half of the cover, arrange the stabilizer with your design sketch plus any lace, ribbon or other trim.

Cut cotton batting to the same size as the cover of the photo pages insert. Cut scraps of colored or patterned fabric that will fit under the reverse appliqué portions of the design. Center the batting under the cover and position the scraps as the middle layer of the sandwich. Pin the layers together to secure.

Step 4

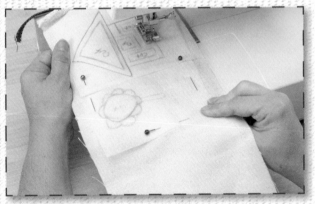

Sew a straight stitch across each short end to secure the turned-under edges. Also sew along any straight lines in the design, such as the walls and roof in the project design. (If you prefer, you can hand-stitch around the design.) The stitching on the design can be as simple or complex as you like. Be sure to stitch around the areas that will be cut away for reverse appliqué. Keep any decorative stitching within the dimensions of the finished album.

Step 5

Sew on any ribbon, lace or other trim, then complete any embroidery or other hand-stitching. Sew on a grouping of buttons as desired, leaving 2" (5cm) clear on the right side for folding the colored fabric.

Step 6

Carefully remove the tear-away stabilizer. To open up the areas for reverse appliqué, start with a seam ripper, then continue with scissors, if needed, to trim away the cover fabric within the stitching lines. Make sure you cut out all the areas where you want the colored fabric to show, and don't worry if the fabric starts to fray—it adds to the charm!

Step 7

Add any final details you want to show on the cover. Here I stitched the word *home* across the roof, replacing the *o* with a button.

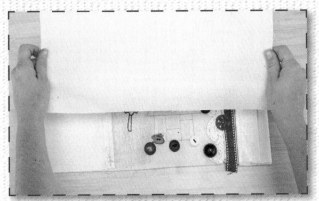

Step 8

Lay the cover piece so the batting is on the bottom and the embellished front faces up. Fold the ends of the fabric over the cover front so the piece ends up measuring about ½" (13mm) longer than the photo pages insert on both ends. One flap will be considerably larger than the other.

Variation of the House Design

Simply rearrange the position of the design elements and use a different selection of buttons and trims to create numerous variations of this simple design.

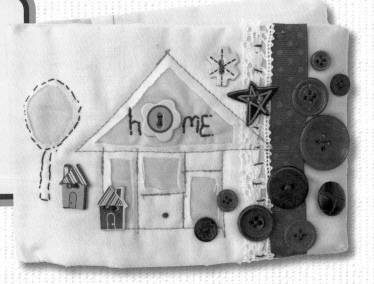

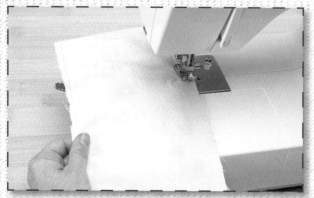

Step 9

Using a ½" (13mm) seam allowance, machine-stitch across the long sides of the fabric/batting sandwich.

Step 10

Remove the pins and turn the album cover right side out.

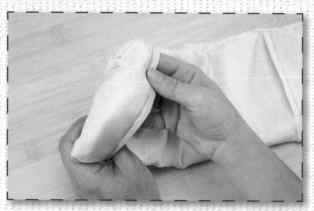

Step 11

Turn the flaps on both ends to create pockets on the inside of the album cover. Slip the covers of the photo pages into these pockets.

Different Shape, Different Design

Look for different sizes of photo album inserts and be creative in your fabric, trim and button choices. Remember that it doesn't take a ton of buttons to have an impact.

PART TWO:
BUTTON STYLE

Previously I mentioned how buttons can make an outfit. When a beautiful jacket catches your eye, it might have more to do with its awesome buttons than the color of the fabric or the style of the jacket itself. It's surprising how such small details can completely change the look and feel of an item.

   This section presents a variety of projects that can really make an outfit shine or at least provide an interesting accent. You'll have fun making them and even more fun showing them off. Along the way, I hope you learn a few tricks to help you expand and transform your wardrobe with only a modest investment. A lot of these projects use recycled materials, which is always a good thing.

SQUID TIE

Know any men who hate to wear ties? If you're like me you do, but this tie will make any tie hater come around.

Start with the squid pattern. Once you see how easy it is to make, you'll be coming up with your own designs. Tie-wearing has never been so much fun.

Designed by Aorta

Materials List

two buttons for eyes

embroidery floss for the eyes

embroidery needle

one 7" × 14" (18cm × 36cm) fabric piece for the squid (color of choice)

one 7" × 14" (18cm × 36cm) piece of iron-on interfacing (I used Heat N Bond Lite)

iron

pencil

scissors

sewing machine

sewing thread

template for squid (page 134)

one tie (3¾" [9cm] or wider ties work best)

waxed paper or press cloth

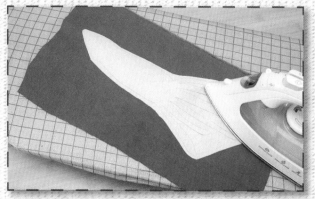

Step 1

Copy the squid template on page 134 enlarged to 196 percent. Trace or copy the shape to the paper side of the iron-on interfacing. Do not cut it out.

Heat the iron to the appropriate setting for the fabric you're using. Iron the interfacing (drawing side up) to the wrong side of the fabric until they bond.

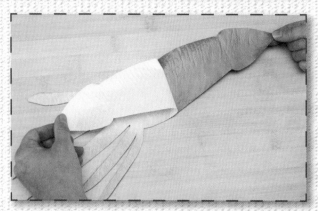

Step 2

Cut out the squid shape, then peel away the paper backing from the interfacing.

Step 3

Position the squid in the desired spot on the tie. Using waxed paper or a press cloth to prevent scorching the tie, iron the squid into place.

Step 4

Once the squid is bonded to the tie, carefully trim away any arms/tentacles that extend beyond the edges of the tie.

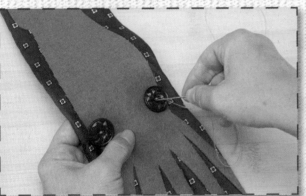

Step 5

Using the presser foot on your sewing machine as a guide, stitch the squid to the tie. Use embroidery floss to sew on the 2 button eyes.

What Color Is Your Squid?

Use your imagination to create a squid never before seen, using a bright fabric color and unusual buttons for the eyes.

FELTED SWEATER HAND WARMERS

Have you ever washed one of your favorite sweaters only to shrink it by mistake? And then you felt so heartbroken that you simply couldn't bear to throw it away!

Now you can turn such accidents into great new winter accessories. With only basic sewing skills, you can whip up these felted wool hand warmers even as the first snowflakes of the season are falling. (See page 58 for an easy scarf to make from sweater leftovers.)

See the tips on page 61 for felting old sweaters and other wool knits.

Designed by Kristen Rask

Materials List

six to eight complementary buttons

needle

scissors

sewing machine

shrunken old sweater (or felted sweater)

straight pins

thread

Step 1

Cut off the sleeves of a shrunken or felted sweater at the shoulder.

Step 2

Cut the cuff from each sleeve.

Step 3

Turn each sleeve inside out and trim away the seam.

Step 4

Using your own hand as a guide, lay your wrist at the end of one sleeve (the end where the cuff had been). Wrap the knit fabric around your hand and pin* it between your thumb and index finger.

Getting a little help from a friend can be useful at this stage so you don't stick yourself.

Step 5

Bring the sides of the knit fabric together at the wrist and pin below the thumb, leaving a space where your thumb can stick out.

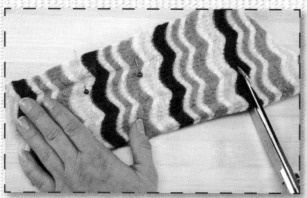

Step 6

Along the top of the hand warmer, cut off the excess fabric so your fingers can stick out; adjust the length according to how short you want the hand warmer to be.

Step 7

Determine a spot that makes the fabric snug against the sides of your fingers and insert a pin; this marks where to sew the upper side seam in the hand warmer.

Step 8

Take off the hand warmer. Machine-sew from the top of the hand warmer down to the first pin above the thumb, stitching where you pinned along the side of the fingers in Step 7 (but don't sew over the pin). Backstitch to secure the seam and cut the thread.

Step 9

Stitch from the pin below the thumb down to the bottom of the hand warmer. Try on the hand warmer to make sure it fits. Trim the excess fabric from the seams you just sewed.

Step 10

Turn the hand warmer right side out. Hand-stitch a vertical row of 3 or 4 buttons running up from the wrist along the outside of the hand warmer.

Repeat Steps 4–9 for the second hand warmer; make sure you reverse the position of the thumb opening.

FELTED SWEATER CUPCAKE SCARF

You can make a matching scarf with a cupcake motif from shrunken sweater pieces left over from the *Felted Sweater Hand Warmers* project (page 52). Or go with other felted knit pieces to create a completely different look. Either way, this scarf is easy to make and snuggly fun to wear.

See tips on page 61 for felting old sweaters and other wool knits.

Designed by Kristen Rask

Materials List

bugle beads (for cupcake sprinkles, optional)

one button for the scarf (for cupcake cherry)

embroidery floss (for cupcake details)

felted sweater remnant from Felted Sweater Hand Warmers *(page 52) or other shrunken knit pieces*

needle

scissors

sewing machine

straight pins

cupcake template pieces (page 134)

thread

wool felt (colors according to the kind of cupcake you're making)

Step 1

From the felted sweater, work from the waist up to cut matching strips about 3½" × 14" (9cm × 36cm) or whatever size you need for the scarf you're planning to make.

Step 2

Pin the cut knit strips end to end, right sides together (or alternate right and wrong sides for a different look). Machine-sew each strip to the next with a straight stitch.

Step 3

Copy the cupcake bottom and top templates from page 134 and cut them out. Use these to cut the cupcake shapes from wool felt.

Hand-stitch the felt cupcake embellishments to the end of the scarf using a backstitch; then add a button to serve as a cherry. Add "sprinkles" by embroidering small straight stitches on the icing part of the cupcake, or sew on beads. Embroider lines on the cupcake bottom.

TIPS & TRICKS

What about working with one of those great sweaters you see in the thrift store? If it's at least 95% wool, buy it! You can felt it (i.e., "shrink" it) just by machine-washing it on a regular setting (add a little detergent and some old towels for extra agitation) and machine-drying on the hottest setting. You'll wind up with a great piece of felted knit that's the ideal weight for making accessories to keep your hands and neck warm all winter long. (If the knit seems a little too open or loose, put it through the washer and dryer again so it will tighten up even more.)

FABRIC COLLAGE JACKET

Have you ever bought a jacket you liked at the store, but when you got it home, you decided it was just a little too boring to wear? This project will transform any jacket into a unique fashion piece you'll be proud to show off.

   Use leftover scraps of fabric for the ship and sails collage, and embellish your design with bits of lace, trim and buttons from your stash. In an afternoon you can turn a blah piece into a head-turning fashion statement. You could easily apply this project to any shirt, jean jacket or tote bag.

Designed by Margaret Oomen

Materials List

vintage buttons (assorted)

decorative ribbon

embroidery floss

embroidery needle

fabric scraps

lace and trim scraps

sewing machine

ship and sails template (page 138)

thread

Step 1

Copy the ship template on page 138 and cut out. Use these pattern pieces to cut shapes from assorted scraps of fabric. For inspiration, see the photo of the back of the sample jacket on page 62. As you lay out the fabric pieces on the back of your jacket, incorporate snippets of lace, other trim and several buttons into your design. (Taking a picture of your design will help you remember where everything will go when you begin to sew.)

Step 2

Machine-sew the individual sails and ship pieces according to your design. Embellish the ship with buttons, trim and embroidery. Don't be afraid to add and change as you go.

Step 3

Machine-sew decorative ribbon around the cuffs of the jacket sleeves and anywhere else you like. See the photo of the front of the sample jacket on page 67 for inspiration.

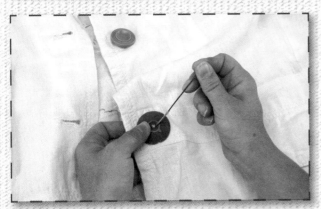

Step 4

Stitch different buttons to the jacket's placket (vintage buttons look really nice here).

Step 5

Embellish the jacket pockets with scraps of fabric, trim and buttons. Here I'm using the blanket stitch to add a piece of ribbon.

Step 6

Add a few buttons to 1 corner of the collar.

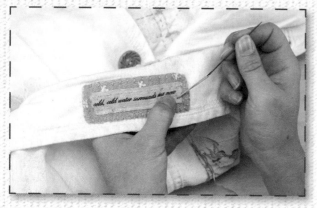

Step 7

Stitch labels that reflect your personal style to the inside and outside of the back of the collar.

Front View

A variety of embellishments, such as vintage buttons, decorative ribbon and touches of embroidery, enhance the jacket rather than overwhelm it.

On Next Page.

CARRY-ME-HOME TOTE BAG

This tote is a recycler's dream, perfect for repurposing old clothes and a used belt or tie. Select more sophisticated fabrics and colors to take this tote from casual to chic.

Designed by Kristen Rask

Materials List

assorted buttons

one 11" × 5¼" (28cm × 13cm) piece of blue cotton fabric (sky)

one 11" × 19½" (28cm × 50cm) piece of printed cotton fabric (lining*)

D rings for strap (optional)

embroidery floss

embroidery needle

iron

one 11" × 6" (28cm × 15cm) piece of linen fabric (ground)

one 11" × 10¼" (28cm × 26cm) piece of linen fabric (tote back)

scissors

sewing machine

silk tie or belt

straight pins

house and cloud templates (page 135)

thread

wool felt (scraps)

*You can use linen for the lining instead, if you like the look.

Step 1

Turn 1 edge of the blue sky piece ¼" (6mm) and steam iron. Lay the sky piece over the linen ground piece with the unturned edge aligned with the edge of the ground piece. Machine-sew the 2 pieces together with a ¼" (6mm) seam using straight stitches.

Step 2

Iron the sky/ground seam flat and spread the piece open. Copy the house and cloud templates on page 135 and cut out. Use the templates to cut shapes from felt. Position the shapes on the sky/ground piece wherever you want them. Hand-stitch the pieces to the fabric using a backstitch around the perimeter of each shape.

Step 3

With 1 strand of floss, add small embroidered details such as the windows and door. Use your favorite embroidery stitches for a personal touch.

Step 4

Lay out a path of buttons from the house and stitch into place; use several stitches for each button to make sure they're secure.

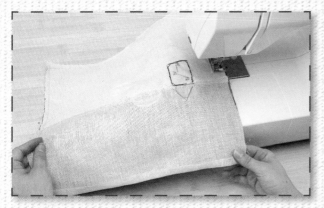

Step 5

When you've finished embellishing the ground/sky piece, sew it to the back piece with right sides facing, leaving about ½" (13mm) of the opening edges unsewn.

Step 6

Clip the corners and turn the bag right side out. Fold the lining piece in half with right sides facing and sew the sides together, leaving about ½" (13mm) of the top edge unsewn.

Step 7

Trim the lining close to the stitched line on each side. Insert the lining into the bag. Fold in the top of both the bag and the lining. Pin the folded edge of the lining to the folded edge of the bag and sew them together around the perimeter of the bag's opening.

Step 8

Cut a silk tie to the length you would like for the strap. Fold the cut edges over and stitch a seam about ½" (13mm) from the ends. (I used D rings on the sample bag to make the strap adjustable.)

Center the tie ends over the inside side seams of the bag and sew together to finish. Backstitch over the stitching to reinforce the hold.

CAMERA CAMERA CASE

No, your eyes aren't playing tricks on you, and that's not a typo in the project title. This camera-shaped camera case is the cutest protection ever for your digital camera.

Use buttons from old shirts or vintage favorites from your stash to really make this project snap.

Designed by Hine Mizushima

Materials List

assorted buttons

crochet hook

embroidery floss

embroidery needle

fabric scraps (for lens pieces)

felt in three different colors (the thicker the felt, the better; or double the layers)

interfacing

sanding block

camera templates on pages 136–137

yarn or cord

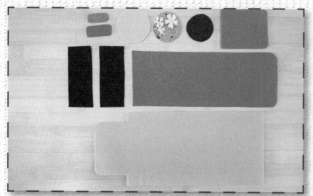

Step 1

Using the templates on pages 136–137, cut the camera pieces from felt and the lens pieces from fabric scraps. Color choices are up to you, but vary them according to the shapes shown in the photo.

Step 2

Hand-stitch the 3 lens parts together. Embroider a running stitch around the inner circumference of the top lens piece.

Step 3

Sew the assembled lens to the camera body slightly off center.

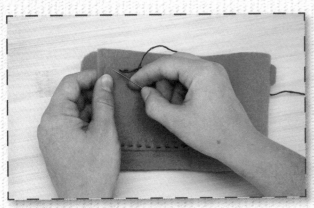

Step 4

Stitch the 2 layers of the flash together, then sew these to the camera body. Also sew the LCD holder to the body.

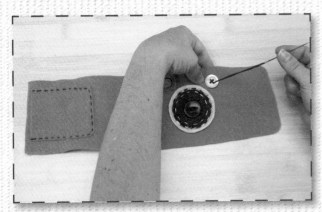

Step 5

Sew 2 buttons, stacked, to the camera body as a viewfinder (eye) and 1 larger button to the lens.

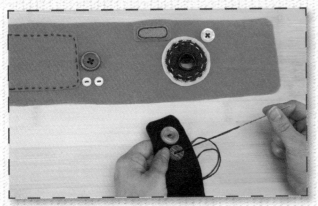

Step 6

Sew 2 small buttons and 1 larger button next to the LCD pocket (these should look like control buttons). When you sew the big button, position an extra piece of felt under the button on the wrong side of the camera body for reinforcement. Sew 2 buttons on the top of the camera to look like on/off and shutter buttons.

Step 7

Sew the camera pieces together. Start by stitching the top piece with the on/off and shutter buttons to the top edge of the body (begin sewing at the LCD pocket).

Step 8

Continue sewing around the other 2 sides of the top piece, rounding the body piece. Snip the thread and tie a knot to secure. Trim the excess thread.

Repeat Steps 7–8 to sew the bottom piece to the lower edge of the camera body.

Step 9

Fold the lining and machine-sew about ⅛" (3mm) from the edges down each side to secure. Stitch across the top corners at the base of the flap, creating triangles.

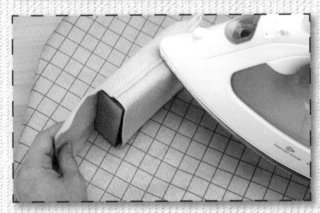

Step 10

Insert the sanding block into the body, and iron the seams flat.

Step 11

Sew diagonally across both bottom corners 12" (30cm) from the points. Iron the seams again. Insert the sanding block again and iron the corners flat against the bottom of the lining.

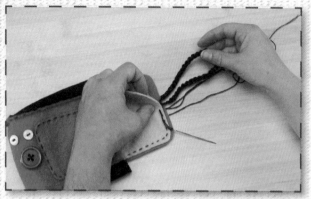

Step 12

Insert the lining into the camera body. The lining flap should be a little shorter than the body flap, so that when the 2 are folded over together, they line up.

Cut a piece of cord or crochet a chain that is about 9½" (24cm) long (if crocheting, leave long tails for sewing). Starting on 1 side of the flap, sew a running stitch around the edge to secure the 2 layers together, but stop when you reach the top center of the flap. Use a needle to insert the cord or the tails of the chain. Apply a bit of fabric glue for extra hold.

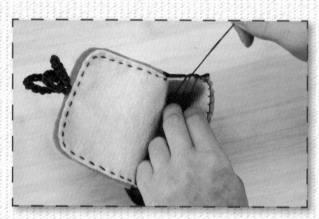

Step 13

Continue stitching around the rest of the flap. To finish the case, sew a blanket stitch around the opening of the case to secure the camera body and lining.

Back View of Case

The green and blue cases use a loop of crocheted chain as a closure, but alternatives like cord are both functional and attractive as well.

Pretty As a Picture

Different colors of felt and fabric and various combinations of buttons make each camera camera case unique.

LAYERED-APPLIQUÉ CLUTCH

One great thing about this clutch is that you can design it to match any outfit. Perfect for a casual night out or a special occasion, the pieces come together quickly. In no time you'll be "clutching" your favorite new accessory.

Designed by Candi Cane-Canncel

Materials List

three aqua buttons (I used La Mode Style #3740)

three aqua 7/16" (1cm) buttons (I used La Mode Style #3623)

two 12½" × 7½" (32cm × 19cm) pieces of woven cotton lining fabric (chocolate brown)

three large and three small ovals* from walnut brown felt

three large and three small ovals* from peacock blue felt

three large and three small ovals* from tan cashmere felt (I used Rainbow Classic Felt for all the oval appliqués)

two 12½" × 7½" (32cm × 19cm) pieces of beige wool felt

two 12½" × 7½" (32cm × 19cm) pieces of heavy-weight interfacing

sewing machine

sewing thread in beige, brown and aqua

one 9" (23cm) brass jeans zipper (I used Coats and Clark, 155 Dogwood)

zipper foot for sewing machine

*Copy the small and large oval templates from page 139.

Step 1

Iron the interfacing to the beige wool felt. Cut several elliptical shapes from the cashmere tan felt and machine appliqué them randomly to the right side of the beige wool felt.

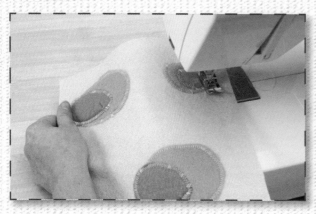

Step 2

Appliqué smaller elliptical peacock blue shapes over the cashmere tan shapes.

Step 3

Appliqué the walnut brown shapes over the peacock blue shapes for the final layer.

Step 4

Also appliqué one 3-layered elliptical shape to the back piece of beige wool felt.

Step 5

Sew 1 button to each layered appliqué as shown.

Step 6

Cut a 11" × 15½" (28cm × 39cm) piece of brown cotton lining fabric. Sew a ¼" (6mm) seam on each of the 11" (28cm) sides.

Step 7

Fold the lining in half, right sides together, and sew each side closed.

Step 8

Center the 9" (23cm) zipper face down along the top edge of 1 beige felt piece.

Step 9

Attach the zipper foot, then sew the first half of the zipper to the beige felt piece, moving the zipper pull as necessary to keep it out of the way of the foot.

Sew the other half of the zipper to the front top edge of the second beige felt piece.

Step 10

With the right sides of the felt still facing, sew the top portion outside of the zipper, and stitch the sides and bottom together. Start at 1 end of the zipper and hold the 2 halves together from the top down to the felt. Then make a 90° turn and sew along the remaining top edge of the felt. Continue down the side and around the rest of the clutch.

When you reach the other end of the zipper, turn again and sew a line perpendicular to the top of the bag to secure the other 2 ends of the zipper together.

Step 11

Notch the corners out, open the zipper and turn the clutch right side out. Insert the lining into the clutch and hand-stitch it to the felt along either side of the zipper.

ZIP IT! POUCH

A zippered pouch has so many uses—and this one is especially unique with button and ribbon embellishments. Make several, and customize each one to fit your uses. A makeup bag, wallet or craft supplies pouch are just some of the options!

Designed by Kristen Rask

Materials List

three to six buttons (varied)

¼ yd (23cm) cotton fabric (lining)

¼ yd (23cm) wool felt

needle

pencil

1' (30cm) ribbon

scissors

sewing machine

straight pins

thread

7" (18cm) zipper

zipper foot for sewing machine

Step 1

Cut two 6" × 7½" (15cm × 19cm) pieces each of wool felt and cotton lining. Cut 9" (23cm) length of ribbon. Pin the ribbon along 1 long side of 1 felt piece about 1" (25mm) from the top edge. Machine-sew the ribbon into place with a straight stitch.

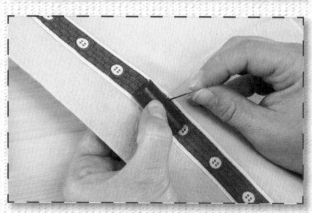

Step 2

Center a decorative button along the ribbon strip and hand-sew into place.

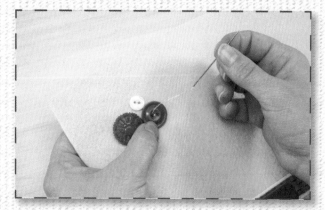

Step 3

Add any other buttons that you want to the clutch. Be sure to place all buttons at least 1" (25mm) in from any edge.

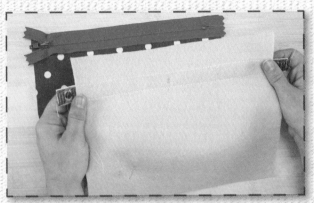

Step 4

Lay the piece of cotton lining right side up on the table. Lay the zipper face down along the top edge of the lining, then lay the felt with the buttons on it right side down. Pin the pieces together.

Step 5

Attach the zipper foot, then machine-sew along the edge that has the zipper first; with the zipper closed, begin just past the pull and continue all the way to the end. Open the zipper a bit and sew together the beginning portion. Make sure you do not sew too close to the zipper so your fabric won't get caught.

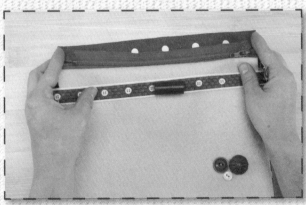

Step 6

Fold the cotton lining back and under the felt piece so that the 2 wrong sides are facing and the unsewn half of the zipper is at the top edge. Lay the other cotton lining piece on the table, then lay the zipper on top of it.

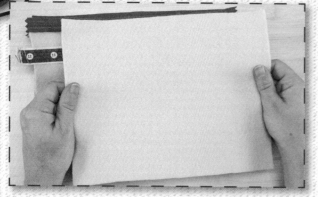

Step 7

Lay the other felt piece on top of the layers.

Step 8

Still using the zipper foot, sew along the top edge to secure the other half of the zipper. Repeat Step 7.

Open the zipper and lay the piece flat with the right sides of the 2 cotton lining pieces together and the 2 right sides of the felt pieces together. Pin in place at the zipper, making sure both ends are folded in the same direction. Sew a seam around the perimeter of the entire piece, starting about 2" (5cm) down from the edge of the cotton lining; this will leave an opening at the end.

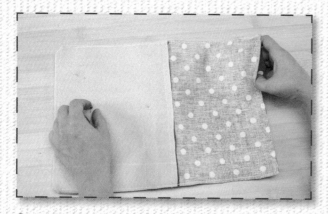

Step 9

Trim the excess fabric except around the opening.

Step 10

Turn the pouch right side out by pulling it through the opening in the cotton lining.

Step 11

Work the fabric out of all of the corners. Use a pencil to push out the corners of the felt. Fold in the excess lining fabric and pin.

Step 12

Sew the opening in the lining shut.

What's Your Style?

Let your preferences and sense of style determine the fabrics and buttons you use.

PART THREE:
BUTTON BLING

My passion for crafting began with the beaded jewelry I created as a child. With so many colors to choose from, the possibilities seemed endless. My affection for combining colors to create unique palettes grew as I continued to experiment.

At some point I became fond of buttons for similar reasons, and thus a relationship with buttons replaced my relationship with beads. That is how the button ring was born (see page 104). Making this simple piece really expanded my world—because of it, I began collecting buttons and making jewelry, and without it, I would not have written this book.

Jewelry is especially fun to make because it can be so diverse. What inspires a piece of jewelry for the workplace is completely different from the inspiration for something worn for a night on the town. It's such a proud feeling when people compliment you on your great necklace or earrings, and you get to say, "I made it."

You'll need a few basic tools and supplies for making button jewelry, all of which you can purchase at your local bead or craft store. Luckily, these tools are fairly inexpensive and can last a lifetime if treated with care. So let's get started. Bring on the button bling!

BLOOMING LEATHER BROOCH

What a great brooch to stick to any hat, jacket, shirt or purse for that extra sparkle. Swap out leather options and button colors for a variety of brooches that you'll wear all week.

Designed by Kristen Rask

Materials List

button of choice (for brooch center)

glue gun

leather glue

leather needle

leather scraps in several different colors

pencil

pin back

scissors

petal template on page 139

Step 1

Trace the button twice on the back of a piece of leather. Cut out each of the traced shapes just outside of the pencil lines.

Step 2

Copy the petal template on page 139. Use this to cut 4 petals from 1 color of leather and 4 petals from a second color. (You may need to adjust the number of petals depending on the size of the button you're using—cut enough petals to go around the circumference of your circle.)

Step 3

Working in a well-ventilated area, use the leather glue according to manufacturer's instructions to adhere the petal shapes to the back of 1 leather circle.

Start with 1 color, applying the bottom end of the petal to the wrong side of the circle, then alternate colors so that 1 color set of petals are at noon, 3, 6 and 9 with the other color set positioned between. When you get to the final petal, tuck the bottom under the bottom of the first petal.

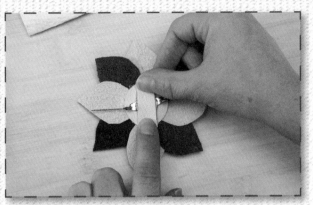

Step 4

Let the glue dry according to the manufacturer's instructions, then sew the button centered on the right side of the leather circle (petal bottoms should be under the circle).

Step 5

With the leather glue, attach the second leather circle to the back of the flower, wrong sides facing, to hide the stitching.

When the glue is dry, use a glue gun to adhere a pin back to the leather circle (make sure the pin back is open). Next, affix a small strip of leather over the open pin back with leather glue to hold the pin in place. Let dry until secure.

The Effect of Different Buttons

Make a whole garden of brooch varieties just by changing out the buttons you use.

KANZASHI-STYLE HAIR CLIP

If you're in need of some new bling for your hair, look no further. This project uses a traditional Japanese approach to make hair ornaments called Kanzashi. Whether you wear a few or just one, you'll definitely have a good hair day.

It may take a little practice to make a nicely formed flower, but it's worth the effort. And what a lovely accessory to make for yourself or friends.

Designed by Thea Starr

Materials List

assorted vintage buttons, preferably with shanks (for the centers)

1" (25mm) cardboard circle (base)

craft glue (clear)

scrap fabric (1 small strip)

five to six 2" (5cm) squares of fabric per flower

1" (25mm) felt circle (for back of base)

hot glue gun

hair clip

pin back or bobby pins (optional)

scissors

Step 1

Make sure the fabric you're using is pressed smooth.
For the first petal, cut out a 2" (5cm) square.

Step 2

Fold the fabric square in half diagonally to make
a triangle.

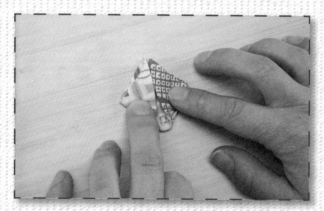

Step 3

Fold both bottom points up to the point of the triangle to
form a diamond.

Step 4

Fold the diamond back along the center (between
creases) to form a new triangle.

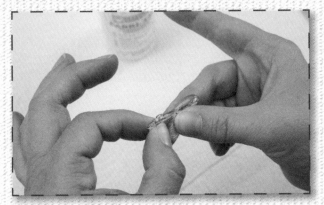

Step 5

Grasp the middle (top) point of the triangle and apply clear craft glue along the straight side to bond all the layers together. Hold until the glue dries and the piece is secure.

Step 6

While still grasping the middle, spread the top up to make a petal shape.

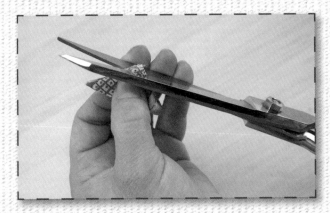

Step 7

Cut the excess material from the center point so that it lies flat.

Step 8

Glue the completed petal to the cardboard circle with the petal point in the center.

Step 9

Repeat Steps 1–8 to make a complete flower. The shape of each petal will determine how many petals you will need to complete a flower.

Step 10

When all of the petals are glued into place, add a generous amount of glue to the center, then insert the button into the glue. (Shank buttons work better; buttons with holes allow excess glue to escape.)

Step 11

Attach the felt circle to the back of the cardboard base using a hot glue gun. Hot glue a hair clip to the felt backing. (For a brooch, simply substitute a pin back for the hair clip.)

Glue a small strip of fabric over the hair clip to conceal the glue and hold the clip in place.

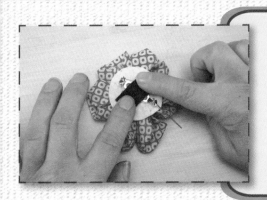

Make a Matching Brooch

The Kanzashi flower also works nicely as a brooch. Simply glue on a pin back instead of a hair clip. Adhere a small strip of fabric over the pin back to hold it in place.

Kanzashi in Bloom

Use different fabrics and buttons for a variety of looks from classy to cute.

EASY BUTTON RING

The origination of this ring marks the start of my button love. Charming and easy to do, this little treasure makes a big impression. You can make it big and chunky if you wish, or keep it small and sweet.

You'll have so much fun making your first button ring, you'll probably go on to design a whole collection.

Designed by Kristen Rask

Materials List

three buttons in graduated sizes and different colors

band elastic (black, or color of choice)

scissors

sewing needle

thread

Step 1

Select 3 buttons in graduated sizes from your stash. I like to pick 3 different colors that go nicely together.

Step 2

To determine the amount of elastic you'll need for your ring size, wrap the elastic around your finger and allow about an extra ¼"–½" (6mm–13mm).

Step 3

Thread a needle with a length of sewing thread, and with it doubled, tie a couple of knots in the end. Holding the elastic with the ends overlapping, begin sewing the band together. Starting at 1 side of the band, sew back and forth from side to side. Then backstitch to the center of the band to finish.

Step 4

Hold the largest button in place over the overlapping part of the elastic. With the needle and thread, secure it by sewing a couple of stitches through the holes.

Step 5

Repeat for the second and the top buttons, securing each with a couple of stitches through the holes.

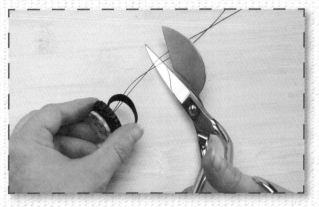

Step 6

Trim the thread, leaving about a 5" (13cm) tail.

Step 7

Tie a square knot with the 2 ends of remaining thread. Trim excess thread to finish.

Fill Your Jewelry Box

Raid your stash and make an entire wardrobe of button rings.

JUST-AS-EASY BUTTON BRACELET

This project is more or less an extension of the button ring project. Make a stand-alone bracelet or a pair that match. Use buttons that are all the same or mix them up. However you design it, this unique wristlet is definitely a conversation piece.

Designed by Kristen Rask

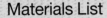

Materials List

assorted buttons

¾"-wide (19mm) black elastic

needle

nylon or quilting thread

scissors

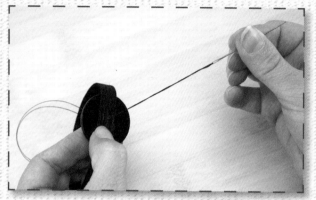

Step 1

Measure elastic to desired length, add ½" (13cm) for seam allowance and cut. (If the bracelet is for yourself, simply measure the circumference of your wrist).

Overlap the ends of the elastic about ½" (13mm) and sew together. Sew on a large button to cover the seam.

Step 2

Stack 1 or 2 smaller buttons on the large button and stitch those down as well. Tie off the thread on the inside of the elastic and trim the excess. Thread the needle with a fresh length of thread and knot the strands together. Position a new button next to the first large button on the elastic. Insert the needle through a hole in the right side of the button down through the elastic and back up through another hole so the knot will be in the hole on the right side of the button.

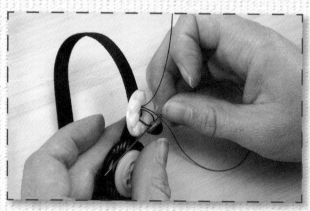

Step 3

Stack 1 or 2 smaller buttons on the new button and stitch them into place. Tie off the thread on the wrong side of the elastic and trim the excess. Thread the needle again, knotting the strands together. Position another new button next to the stacked button you just sewed. Sew this button in place as instructed in Step 2, then stack and sew on 1 or 2 more buttons. Pull the thread taut, then knot and trim the thread on the wrong side of the elastic.

Step 4

Continue to sew, stack and stitch buttons until the elastic is full.

WHEN USING SHANK BUTTONS

If you add a small button with a shank to the top of a stacked set, sew loosely through the shank a couple of times on the first round so you can sew through easily a second time.

Accessorize!
Select buttons with different colors and textures for an earthy, vintage or retro feel.

BUTTON LEATHER EARRINGS

Leather is an attractive background for these dangly earrings. It lends a natural, rustic feel to the work. Play with leather colors and button textures to come up with something that really express your style.

Designed by Kristen Rask

Materials List

arch punch (I use Osborne; their punches come in various diameters. Choose the size you like. I used a 1" [25mm] hole punch for the project sample)

one to three buttons per earring (if using more than one, make sure they range in sizes so they sit on top of each other nicely)

cutting pad (I use Osborne)

two earring hooks*

glover (leather) needle

two jump rings*

leather glue

leather scraps

mallet

needle-nose pliers

sheet of marble to fit under the cutting pad

self-centering punch set (I use the ¹⁄₁₆" [2mm] punch from the Osborne set)

stick or cotton swab

strong thread such as nylon or quilting thread

*use the same kind of metal for the jump rings and hooks

Step 1

Lay a sheet of marble on your work surface with the cutting pad on top for added protection. Using the arch punch and a mallet, punch out 4 circles of leather or suede.

Step 2

Punch a small hole about ⅜" (1cm) from the edge of 1 leather circle. Use this as a template to punch a matching hole into the second leather circle. Repeat the process for the other 2 leather pieces. Using the glover needle, sew each button to the center of a leather circle, inserting the needle from back to front.

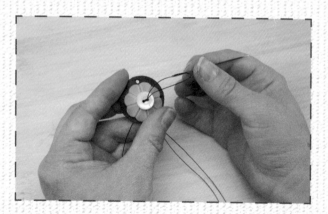

Step 3

If sewing on more than 1 button, stitch each several times to secure, starting with the bottom, largest button.

Step 4

Trim the thread, leaving about a 5" (13cm) tail. Tie the 2 strands of thread into a knot at the back of the leather circle and trim.

Step 5

When buttons have been sewn to each of the 2 leather circles, apply a small amount of leather glue to the wrong side of the remaining 2 leather circles (the ones without buttons). I use a stick or cotton swab to spread the glue, making sure not to get it in the punched hole.

Position each circle with buttons on top of a glued circle, aligning the punched holes. Wipe off any excess glue right away. Let it dry according to maufacturer's instructions.

Step 6

Using needle-nose pliers, open a jump ring and insert it through the punched hole in one of the earrings.

Close the jump ring. Open the loop on the ear wire and attach it. (See photo below for finished appearance.)

Repeat for the second earring.

Make a Statement

Have a pair of "statement" buttons in your stash? They'd be perfect as a pair of earrings!

BOOMBOX PIN

If you are a child of the seventies and eighties, the boombox will always have a special place in your heart. Sport your love for the old school way by making your very own boombox pin. Viva la Boombox!

Designed by Kristen Garland

Materials List

acrylic paint (silver)

adhesive (appropriate for use with polymer clay)

two round buttons (for boombox speakers)

one package polymer clay (white)

craft knife

cutting blade or thin ruler

paintbrush

pin back

one fine-point permanent marker in a contrasting color

roller

fine-grit sandpaper (or an emery board)

sewing needle

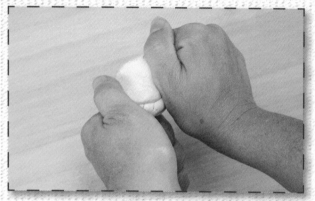

Step 1

Condition about half of a package of white polymer clay by working it in your hands. Using a roller and a cutting blade or a thin ruler, shape the worked clay into a rectangle that is about ¼" × 2¼" × ¼" (6mm × 6cm × 6mm). Reserve a tiny amount of clay for the boombox handle, buttons and cassette window.

Step 2

Roll 2 tiny pieces of clay into balls about the size of cooked tapioca. Score 1 side of each using a craft knife, then lightly press each onto 1 long side of the rectangle as pictured.

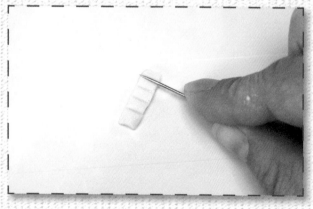

Step 3

To create the cassette window and control buttons, roll out a thin bit of clay. Use the blade of a craft knife to cut a small rectangle for the cassette window and a strip for the controls.

   Press the side of a needle 4 times into the clay strip to divide it into 5 buttons (*record*, *play*, *rewind*, *fast-forward* and *stop*), but don't pierce the clay. Set aside the strip and cassette window pieces.

Step 4

To make a handle for the boombox, roll out a small snake of clay about 3" (8cm) long. Create a 90° bend at each end of the snake.

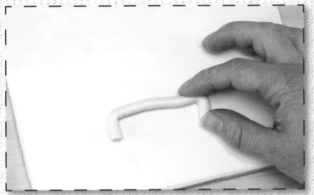

Step 5

Score the ends of the rolled handle, then gently press the handle into the top side of the boombox. Also score the backs of the window and the button strip pieces; lightly press those on the front center of the boombox.

Step 6

For the speakers, lightly press and remove the 2 buttons; you will glue these on after the clay bakes.

Step 7

Bake the formed clay according to the package directions (typically 275° F [135° C], 15 minutes for each ¼" [6mm] of clay thickness). You might need to place a small ball of aluminum foil underneath the handle of the boombox for added support while baking.

Once the boombox has cooled, use sandpaper or an emory board to smooth out any imperfections. Paint the piece with silver acrylic paint except for the strip of play buttons below the window. Two coats offer the best coverage.

Step 8

With a fine-point permanent marker, add the symbols for *pause*, *stop*, *rewind*, *fast-forward* and *play* on the control buttons (refer to the Boombox Button Legend at right).

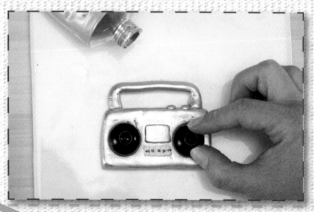

Step 9

Glue the buttons for the speakers into the indentations on the front.

Step 10

When the adhesive has set for the buttons, turn the piece over and glue on a pin back. Let it dry completely.

Old School Style

Style your pin like the boombox that brings back the best memories.

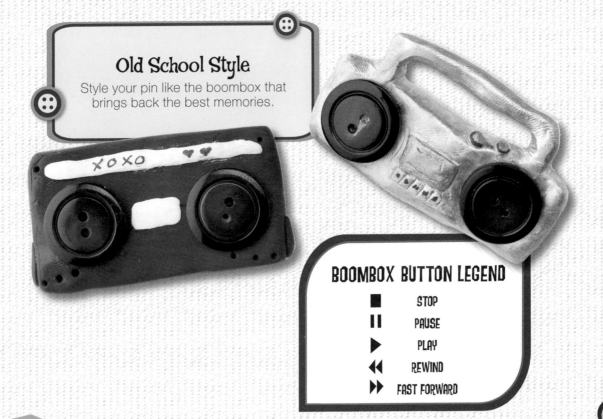

BOOMBOX BUTTON LEGEND

■	STOP
❚❚	PAUSE
▶	PLAY
◀◀	REWIND
▶▶	FAST FORWARD

FELTED BALL BUTTON

Needle felting, also called dry felting, is the process of turning wool fiber into felt using barbed needles. (Industrial felt is made using thousands of these needles.) The felting needle is punched or pushed repeatedly through the wool, which locks the fibers together, creating a matted fabric or three-dimensional object.

These awesome needle-felted buttons make great accessories for a special outfit, or you can turn them into a terrific pair of earrings.

Designed by Moxie

Materials List

4" (10cm) 18-gauge craft wire

one to two felting needles (38g star needles work nicely)

piece of foam rubber (for foam felting mat)

needle-nose pliers

wire cutters

wool roving, ⅛ oz. (4g) each of tangerine, bubblegum and cream

(I used Corriedale wool because it's soft to the touch)

Step 1

With needle-nose pliers, cut about a 2" (5cm) length of wire. Make a loop in the center of each length, then bend and clip the sides out 90°. The looped portion should measure approximately ¼" (6mm).

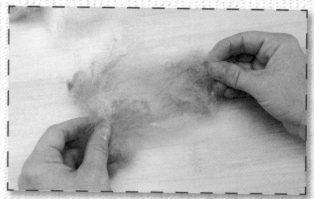

Step 2

Gently pull a tuft about 1½" (4cm) long from each of the 3 colors of wool roving. To create a randomly swirled pattern of color, pinch and pull the wool apart, then mix the 3 colors together as if you were pulling taffy.

Step 3

When the colors are mixed to your satisfaction, roll the blended wool into a relatively compact ball, incorporating the wire button loop with the round part of the loop extending about ⅛" (3mm) beyond the wool.

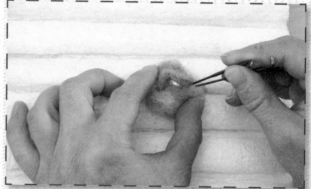

Step 4

Set the loop of the wire in the foam felting mat. Gently poke the fiber from all sides with the felting needle; this will tighten the ball and help it hold its shape. Lift and move the ball often as you work with the needle so you don't attach the wool ball to the foam. Don't worry about the needle hitting the metal loop inside.

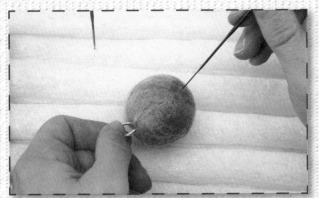

Step 5
Continue to move and poke the ball from all sides. The more you poke, the smaller and denser the ball will become. If it gets too small, blend in some more wool, loosely wrap it around the ball and keep poking. Stop when the ball is the diameter and density you want.

Felt it Up
Don't stop with the button ball: experiment to create buttons in various styles, shapes and colors.

FELTED BUNNY BUTTON

Basically this project is a recipe for creating your own stylized buttons. Break out your scraps of felt, your needle-felting supplies and your imagination. Soon you'll be replacing all of the commercial buttons on your clothing with handmade varieties of your very own.

The instructions that follow result in the bunny button in the photo, left. If you wish to make the matching carrot button, simply follow the same procedures for felting but use orange and green roving and the photo as a reference for shaping the design.

Designed by Moxie

Materials List

button form

felt (craft or wool)

felting needles

piece of foam (for felting pad)

wool roving in white and black (and orange and green, if making the carrot button)

Step 1

Using a felting needle, create a series of holes around the button form through the background piece of commercial felt.

Step 2

Trim the felt about ½" (13mm) outside of the punched line. Tear off a very small amount of roving and form it into a bunny-like shape with your fingers. Center the shape on the felt, then poke all over the shape to lock the fibers in the felt and give the bunny more definition.

Step 3

Continue poking and shaping with the needle, periodically lifting the felt from the foam pad so you don't connect it to the foam. (This is important to remember: If you don't occasionally lift the felt, you'll sadly discover that your bunny is felted to the foam and is impossible to remove without damage.)

Step 4

When the bunny body is finished, add 2 teeny balls of roving for a head and a tail. To add an eye to the head, roll up a miniscule amount of black roving and felt it into position with the needle.

Step 5

Add 2 small oblong shapes of roving for ears and 2 small balls of roving for feet. Finish needle felting all the parts until you're satisfied with the final result.

Step 6

Center the button form over the felted bunny, using the holes punched in Step 1 as a guide. Fold the excess felt to the inside of the form.

Step 7

Push the back of the button form into the wrapped half to finish.

Variations

With your newfound needle-felting skills, the possibilities for cute buttons are only limited by the imagination.

SOLDERED BUTTON RING

This is a hot project in more ways than one. Practice first with the soldering iron and butane torch before attempting this special button ring. In no time your skills will rise to the occasion, and your family and friends will be calling for more.

Designed by Lyndsay Brown

Materials List

anti flux

bezel wire

burnisher

butane torch

glass buttons

small clamp with base

precut Cubitron abrasive discs

easy solder

file

flux

gloves

mug of water

pickling solution

respiratory mask

safety goggles

sandpaper or Dremel Multipurpose Tool

fine-tip permanent marker

20- or 22-gauge sheet metal

soldering block

silver soldering pickle (optional)

sterling silver band (choose your own size)

tin snips or jeweler's saw

torch

wire cutters

Step 1

If your button has a shank, cut it off with wire cutters. Smooth the back with sandpaper or a Dremel. Don't be too aggressive or you'll break the button.

Wrap the circumference of the button with flat bezel wire. Mark where to cut with a fine-tip permanent marker. Cut the wire. **Note:** The bezel setting must fit the button exactly. If it's too loose, the button will not be secure; too tight and it will not fit into the setting.

Step 2

Hold the wire in a clamp and brush a bit of flux over the seam in the bezel. Add a small amount of solder over the seam. If you apply too much flux, rinse, dry and repeat. You can also apply antiflux to protect areas that you want to remain solder-free.

Step 3

Trace the bezel on a piece of sheet metal. Cut the circle out with either tin snips or a jeweler's saw, or use a precut Cubitron abrasive disc.

SAFETY WHILE SOLDERING

Wear a respiratory mask and safety goggles while soldering. Also wear gloves to protect your hands from burns with the torch. Keep a mug of water nearby for cooling the piece after soldering.

Step 4

Use a torch to liquefy the solder and spread it around to join. If you need to solder a second time, you must clean the piece in a soldering pickle (silver). **Important:** When using the pickle, wear protective gear and work in a well-ventilated area with a fan.

Step 5

Cool the hot piece in a mug of water. When the piece is cool enough to touch, dry it and make sure that it fits the button before moving on.

Place the setting face down on a soldering block and measure the middle point for ring placement. Place the bezel wire on the metal disc; confirm that it is completely flush to the disc. Once you have marked the center, hold the ring band to the back of the setting and secure with metal fingers to solder. Apply flux to the border of the disc on the inside of your setting. Use your torch to solder the same way as in Steps 5–7.

Step 6

File any excess solder off the ring and finish the silver as you desire. Polish the piece with pickling solution or fine sandpaper.

Insert the glass button into the bezel and set it; make sure you do not set it unevenly. Once the button is set, smooth the bezel around the button with a burnishing tool. For extra fancy finishing, use a tumbler to polish and smooth your ring.

TEMPLATES

CUPCAKE TEMPLATE

For the *Felted Sweater Cupcake Scarf*, page 58. Actual size.

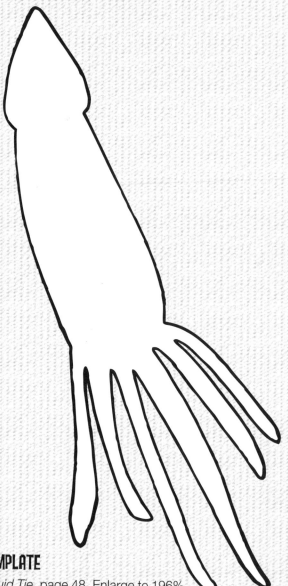

SQUID TEMPLATE

For the *Squid Tie*, page 48. Enlarge to 196%.

CLOUD TEMPLATE

For *Carry-Me-Home Tote Bag*,
page 68. Actual size.

HOUSE TEMPLATE

For the *Carry-Me-Home Tote Bag*,
page 68. Actual size.

CAMERA CASE TEMPLATE

For *Camera Camera Case*,
page 72. Enlarge to 233%.

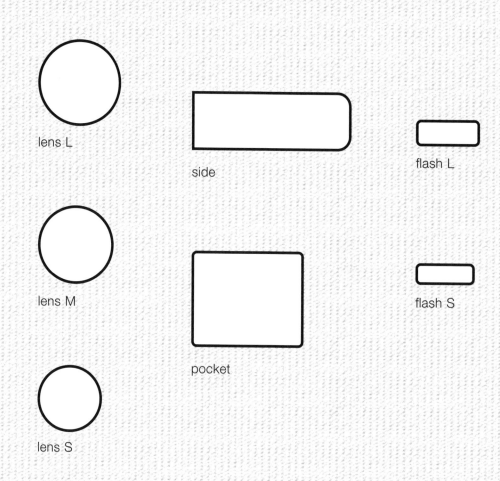

lens L

side

flash L

lens M

pocket

flash S

lens S

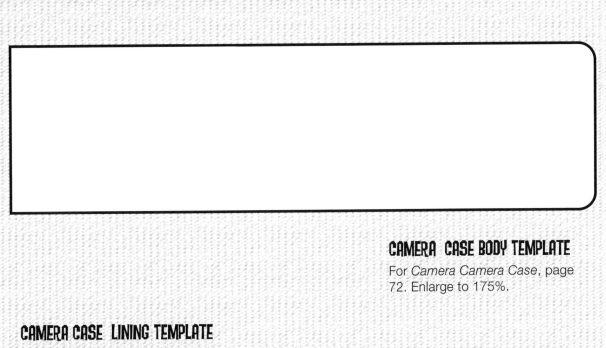

CAMERA CASE BODY TEMPLATE

For *Camera Camera Case*, page 72. Enlarge to 175%.

CAMERA CASE LINING TEMPLATE

For *Camera Camera Case*, page 72. Enlarge to 175%.

SHIP AND SAILS TEMPLATE

For the *Fabric Collage Jacket*, page 62. Enlarge to 200%.

PETAL TEMPLATE

For *Blooming Leather Brooch*, page 94. Actual size.

SMALL OVAL TEMPLATES

For *Layered-Appliqué Clutch*, page 80. Actual size.

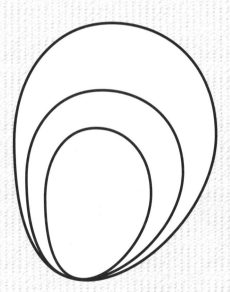

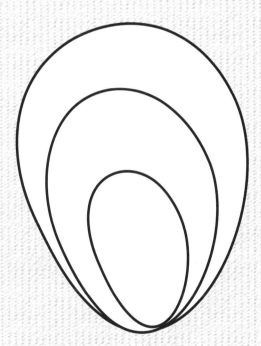

MEDIUM OVAL TEMPLATES

For *Layered Appliqué Clutch*, page 80. Actual size.

LARGE OVAL TEMPLATES

For *Layered Appliqué Clutch*, page 80. Actual size.

WHERE TO FIND BUTTONS

My obsession with buttons started with a bag I purchased at a thrift store. Unfortunately, going to a thrift store does not guarantee you'll find a bag full of buttons, but there are plenty of sources to check.

Start with your local fabric and craft stores. Often you can find bags of basic buttons for sale as well as some really interesting novelty buttons.

Online auctions such as eBay offer some amazing collections, including vintage treasures from "grandma's old button collection." You might have to fight to be the winning bidder, but there are some true diamond-in-the-rough discoveries in auction lots.

As more and more crafters and artists use Etsy, a lot of folks are cleaning out their crafty closets and selling supplies online. A simple search can bring forth the opportunity to buy wonderful buttons.

I am finding more and more button collections at antique stores. Obviously they know the value of such collections, but there are still some lucky finds there!

Don't forget to reclaim buttons from clothing you're about to discard, and check with relatives for forgotten collections of buttons in jars and tins. Such treasure hunts can turn up some real gems.

CONTRIBUTORS

LYNDSAY BROWN turned her passion for jewelry into the business Idle Hands Designs in 2006. She loves to take something from the past and create something new.

PAMELA DAVIS sells her MuchoDesign creations at www.muchodesign.etsy.com and www.muchodesign.com. She lives very happily in Seattle with her cat.

CATHIE FILIAN is the creator, producer and cohost of *Creative Juice* and *Witch Crafts* on the HGTV and DIY Networks. Before *Creative Juice*, Cathie created costumes for major motion pictures. She lives in Los Angeles with her husband, Eddie, and their dog Max.

KRIS GARLAND, a.k.a. Rakka, helped make some of the floral displays for the funeral scenes in the film *21 Grams*. She currently lives in Seattle with her boyfriend and four cats.

CAROL GRILO is an architect who creates bags for her brand, FofysFactory. She lives happily with her husband, Ivan, her cat, Beterraba, and four Blythe dolls.

LISA JORDAN is a rural Minnesota artist whose creations reflect her love of nature and focus on craftsmanship and sustainability.

HINE MIZUSHIMA was born in Japan and now lives in Vancouver, Canada. She's an illustrator, (slow) crafter, plush artist, Etsy seller and a PSMAVA (Puppet-Stop-Motion-Animation-Video-Artist).

MOXIE is a part-time crafter who enjoys crocheting, knitting ("sort of"), making jewelry and doing "a lot of other stuff I can't think of right now." Read her blog, Creative Explosion by Moxie, at http://creativeexplosionbymoxie.blogspot.com.

MARGARET OOMEN is a self-taught crafter, family doctor and mother of four. She blogs at www.resurrectionfern.typepad.com and has an Etsy shop at www.etsy.com/shop.php?user_id=5052132.

JESSICA WYNNE PLYMATE founded Aorta Apparel and lives in Lincoln, Nebraska, with a spastic dachshund, a mountain of fabric and a cherished stash of vintage buttons.

BARBARA PRONSATO works in Seattle in her home studio making laptop sleeves for computer fashionistas. View her work at www.mintika.com

THEA STARR lives in Woodinville, Washington, with her husband and four children as well as a garage full of crafting supplies. She loves trees, gardening and beachcombing.

JACQUELINE YEO of Singapore is the mother of two children, works as an architect and loves anything crafty. She blogs at www.gracierei.blogspot.com.

ABOUT KRISTEN

Kristen Rask has been making handmade gifts, tokens, decorations and jewelry for as long as she can remember. She realized she might be able to make money with her craft after summer camp in 1985; since then she has made a wide variety of crafts using various materials and techniques. "Whether the end result is totally ridiculous or kind of awesome, the end result is never as important as the fun and excitement I get from the creative process," Kristen says, although she does love it more when the end result is awesome.

In Seattle, Kristen owns and operates a boutique called Schmancy where she sells her handmade collection and those of other crafters and artists. Find out more about Kristen, her store and the annual show she curates at www.plushyou.blogspot.com.

Kristen is an avid button collector, although she's a little embarrassed about it, especially when it comes time to move. "Then my friends kind of hate me and my buttons." She hopes this book will inspire you to begin your own love affair with buttons and to create many beautiful gifts and crafts.

INDEX

WANT MORE BUTTON PROJECTS? CHECK OUT THESE OTHER F+W MEDIA TITLES!

BUSY WITH BUTTONS

Jill Gorski

Buttons become the focus in this collection of quick and easy projects for gifts, home décor and accessories. Button history, material identification, care, use and more are also covered.

Paperback, 128 pages, #Z2800
ISBN-10: 0-89689-732-X
ISBN-13: 978-0-89689-732-8

A PASSION FOR BUTTONS!

Stephanie Bourgeois

Step-by-step instructions and clear diagrams make it easy to use buttons of all shapes, sizes and materials (from mother-of-pearl to leather) to create unique art jewelry items.

Paperback, 64 pgs, #Z0895
ISBN-10: 0-7153-2652-X
ISBN-13: 978-0-7153-2652-7

BRACELETS, BUTTONS & BROOCHES

Jane Davis

Use basic beadwork to create beaded accessories to adorn your wardrobe or wrist, or to create a gift. Follow the 200+ step-by-step illustrations to bead your way through 24 projects.

Paperback, 128 pgs, #Z1354
ISBN-10: 0-89689-581-5
ISBN-13: 978-0-89689-581-2

These and other fine North Light titles are available from your local bookstore, craft supply store, online retailer or visit our website at www.mycraftivitystore.com.